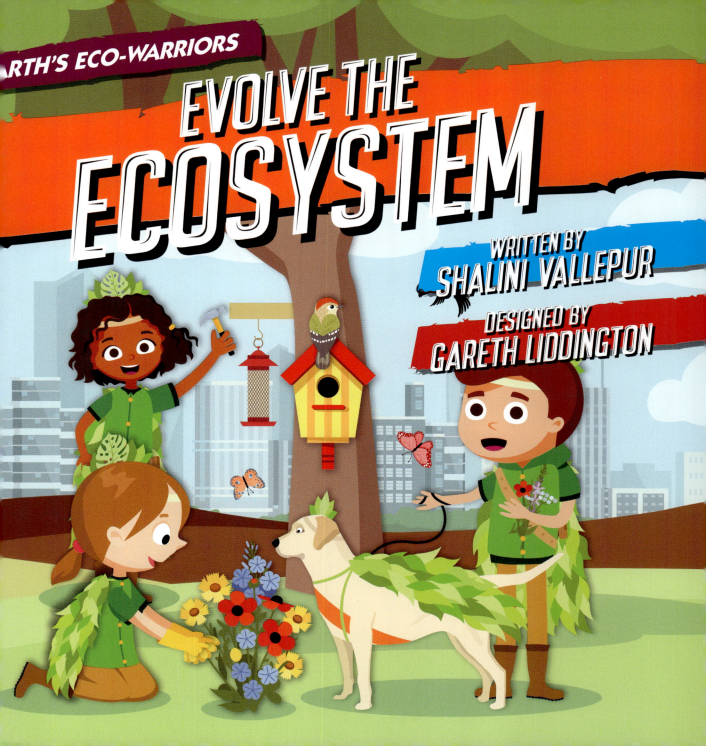

The Planet Promise
I promise to:

Rethink what I use and buy.
Refuse what I don't need.
Reduce my waste and carbon footprint.
Reuse things when I can.
Recycle as much as I can.
Rot food in a <u>compost bin</u>.
Repair broken things.

Earth's Eco-Warriors are <u>evolving</u> the ecosystem. But what does this mean? An ecosystem is a group of living and non-living things, such as plants and rocks, in an area. From soil and sunlight to plants and animals, all the things in an ecosystem need one another. But we are in danger of hurting, or even losing, some ecosystems. We must change and grow, or evolve, the ecosystems around us to help the planet and all living things.

www.littlebluehousebooks.com

Copyright © 2025 by Little Blue House, Mendota Heights, MN 55120. All rights reserved. No part of this book may be reproduced or utilized in any form or by any means without written permission from the publisher.

Little Blue House is distributed by North Star Editions: sales@northstareditions.com | 888-417-0195

Library of Congress Control Number: 2024936732

ISBN
979-8-89359-003-6 (hardcover)
979-8-89359-013-5 (paperback)
979-8-89359-033-3 (ebook pdf)
979-8-89359-023-4 (hosted ebook)

Printed in the United States of America
Mankato, MN
082024

Eco-words that look like <u>this</u> are explained on page 24.

It's a good idea to put some rocks and clay pots around the pond too. This helps frogs easily get into and out of the water, and it gives them more places to hide from <u>predators</u>.

Over the next few weeks, Earth's Eco-Warriors evolved the yard. Because they had planted flowers, composted food scraps, and made a milkweed garden, the yard's ecosystem was slowly evolving. More living things moved in.

DO YOU REMEMBER WHAT THE YARD LOOKED LIKE BEFORE IT WAS EVOLVED? TURN BACK TO PAGE 4 TO TAKE A LOOK!

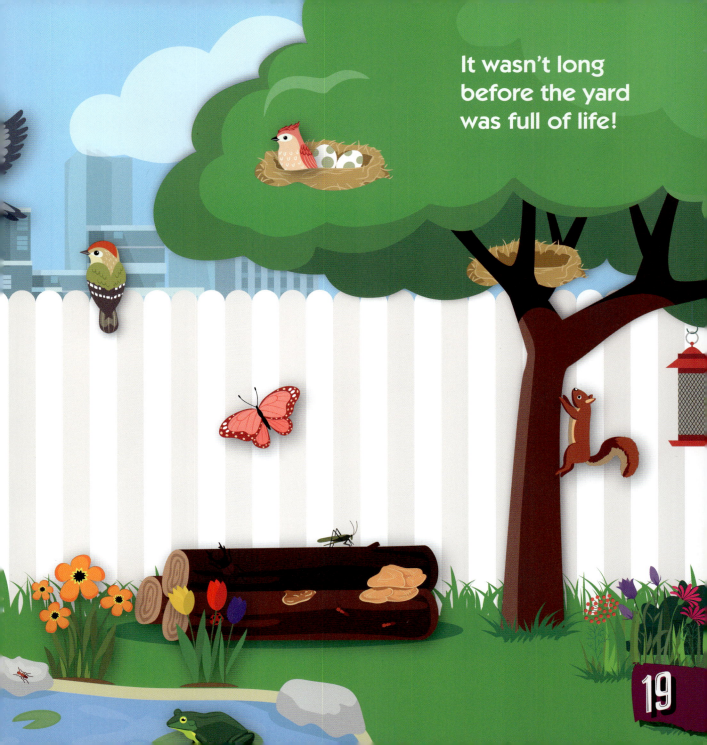

While Pietro's yard was busy evolving, Bailey wanted to help the living things where she lived. With the help of her mom, Bailey set up bird feeder on the balcony of her apartment.

She also bought clay pots and planted beautiful flowers to help the bees and butterflies in the city.

IT DOESN'T MATTER WHERE YOU LIVE. EVERYBODY CAN DO THINGS TO HELP EVOLVE THE ECOSYSTEM.

ACTIVITY: BUILD A BUG HOTEL

Would you like to evolve the ecosystem like Earth's Eco-Warriors? Let's make a bug hotel for bugs to live in! Don't forget to ask an adult to help.

THINGS YOU WILL NEED

- Old wooden planks or wooden pallets
- Old roof tiles
- Dry leaves, dead wood, sticks, and moss
- Small, old logs
- Clay pots
- Big and small stones
- Bricks with holes

DON'T FORGET TO PROTECT YOUR HANDS WITH GARDENING GLOVES.

ECO-WORDS

attract	To make something or someone want to come closer.
compost bin	A special bin where yard waste and some food scraps turn into soil.
endangered	When a type of animal is in danger of dying out forever.
environment	The natural world.
evolving	When something slowly changes.
food bin	A bin that is for food waste.
fungi	Simple living things that are not plants or animals.
habitats	The natural areas where animals and plants live.
nutrient-rich	When something is full of the things that plants and animals need in order to grow and stay healthy.
pesticides	Things that are used to kill the insects that damage plants.
pests	Animals, plants, or fungi that can damage or cause trouble in an area.
predators	Animals that hunt other animals for food.
rot	When something breaks down and decays.

INDEX

bees, 8, 21
birds, 6, 9–12, 20
bug hotels, 22–23
butterflies, 4–5, 8, 14, 21
compost, 2, 12–14, 18
ecosystems, 2–3, 5, 8–9, 18, 21–22
flowers, 8, 13, 16, 18, 21
habitats, 5–6, 8, 14
nests, 10
Planet Promise, 2–3, 13
plants, 2, 8–9, 13, 16
ponds, 6, 16–17
rocks, 2, 17
trees, 6, 10

PHOTO CREDITS

Cover & Throughout – Olga1818, art.tkach, SofiaV, tn-prints, Grat Vishenka, Pretty Vectors, 2&3 – Inspiring, 4&5 – Laia Design Lab, Eloku, Maquiladora, NotionPic, Park Sun, Lorelyn Medina, Kaimen, Igdeeva Alena, Viktorija Reuta, IconBunny, 6&7 – mary rodyukova, Panda Vector, Visual Generation, Dzm1try, Oksana Alekseeva, tn-prints, Alfmaler, 8&9 – belander, Sudowoodo, kelttt, MicroOne, 10&11 – Vectors Bang, kup1979, Lana_Samcorp, vectorOK, uiliaaa, 12&13 – ksuklein, 14&15 – Studio_G, HappyPictures, 20&21 – Elvetica, Pogorelova Olga, MicroOne, 22&23 – Lora Sutyagina, legdrubma.

Images are courtesy of Shutterstock.com. With thanks to Getty Images, Thinkstock Photo, and iStockphoto.

All facts, statistics, web addresses, and URLs in this book were verified as valid and accurate at the time of writing. No responsibility for any changes to external websites or references can be accepted by either the author or the publisher.